AF576423

This book is a gift for

From

Date

On the occasion of

God's Love for Us

Bible Stories for Children

Redemptorist Pastoral Publication
Illustrated by Lula Guzmán

Imprimi Potest: Stephen T. Rehrauer, CSsR, Provincial Denver Province, the Redemptorists.
Published by Liguori Publications, Liguori, Missouri 63057.

Imprimatur: In accordance with CIC 827, permission to publish has been granted on June 22, 2020, by the Most Reverend Mark S. Rivituso, Auxiliary Bishop, Archdiocese of St. Louis. Permission to publish is an indication that nothing contrary to Church teaching is contained in this particular work. It does not imply any endorsement of the opinions expressed in the publication, or a general endorsement of any author; nor is any liability assumed by this permission.

To order, visit Liguori.org or call 800-325-9521.

p ISBN: 978-0-7648-2840-9
e ISBN: 978-0-7648-7192-4

Cataloging-in-Publication data is on file with the Library of Congress.

Liguori Publications, a nonprofit corporation, is an apostolate of the Redemptorists.
To learn more about the Redemptorists, visit Redemptorists.com.

Printed in the United States of America
24 23 22 21 20 / 5 4 3 2 1
First Edition

Introduction

Many years ago, God gave some people the mission of writing a very special book: the Bible. Through it, God shared his message of love with us. In its pages, you will find teachings and many lessons that will help you know and love God better. It will help you learn what makes God happy and how you can teach others by your example. May these biblical stories, drawn and retold for children, help you—no matter how old you are—to grow closer to God and also to Jesus, his beloved Son.

Table of Contents

The Old Testament

Introduction to the Old Testament 12
The Creation of the World 14
The Creation of Adam and Eve 16
Original Sin 18
Noah's Ark 20
Abraham's Faith 22
The Sacrifice of Isaac 24
Moses' Childhood 26
The Israelites Cross the Red Sea. 28

The Ten Commandments 30

The Golden Calf 32

David and Goliath 34

The Wisdom of Solomon 36

The Prophets 38

The New Testament

Introduction to the New Testament 40

The Annunciation 42

The Birth of Jesus 44

The Magi 46

The Killing of the Innocent Children 48

Jesus Teaches in the Temple 50

Jesus' Baptism 52

The Wedding at Cana. 54

Jesus Calls His Disciples 56

The Resurrection of Lazarus 58

Jesus Calms a Storm 60

The Multiplication of the Bread and Fish 62

The Lord's Prayer. 64

Jesus Throws the Merchants Out of the Temple 66

The Parable of the Prodigal Son. 68

Jesus Is the Good Shepherd 70

Jesus Enters Jerusalem 72

The Last Supper 74

The Prayer in the Garden 76

Judas' Betrayal 78

The Crown of Thorns. 80

The Crucifixion 82

Jesus' Body Is Taken Down from the Cross 84

The Resurrection 86

Jesus Appears to the Disciples. 88

The Disciples of Emmaus 90

The Ascension into Heaven 92

The Coming of the Holy Spirit 94

The Old Testament

Introduction to the Old Testament

From the creation of the first human beings, long before Jesus came to earth, God, the Father, wanted to be near us. In fact, he created us to be his friends. That's what the Old Testament is about. It is the first part of the Bible, which tells the story of friendship between God and us, as begun with his Chosen People of Israel. We hear the story of the hard times and threats that they had to overcome to arrive in the land promised to them by God. The Old Testament also tells about the men and women God chose to guide and lead his people. We learn about the prophets, who brought God's message to us. We see how, even though his people made many mistakes, God still loved them and continued to be their friend. He was preparing them for the coming of his Son, Jesus Christ.

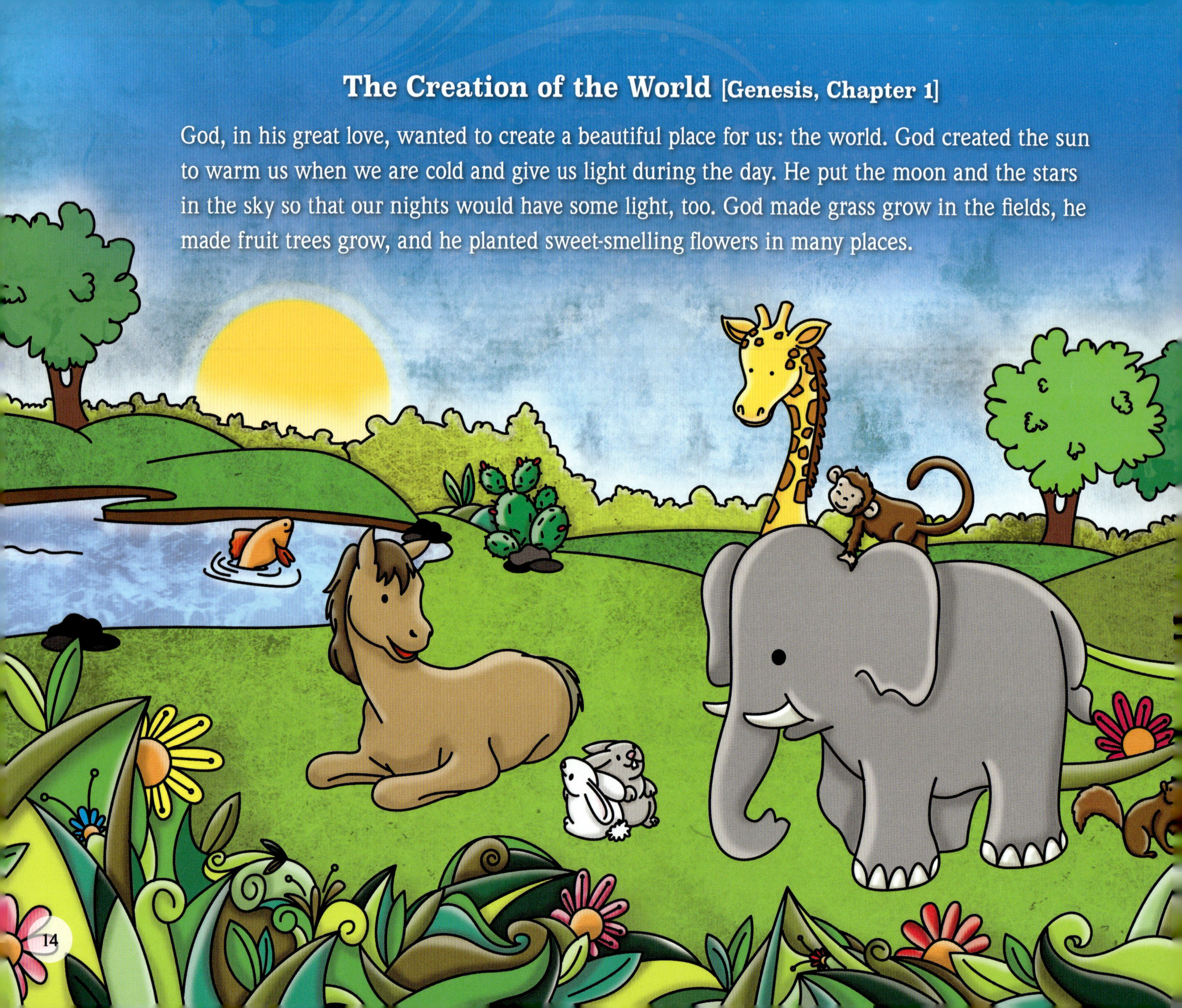

The Creation of the World [Genesis, Chapter 1]

God, in his great love, wanted to create a beautiful place for us: the world. God created the sun to warm us when we are cold and give us light during the day. He put the moon and the stars in the sky so that our nights would have some light, too. God made grass grow in the fields, he made fruit trees grow, and he planted sweet-smelling flowers in many places.

He filled the sky with birds, the earth with animals, and the water with fish. He gave them all the food that they needed. God created a good world in which everything was beautiful. He lovingly shared it with us so we could take care of it for him.

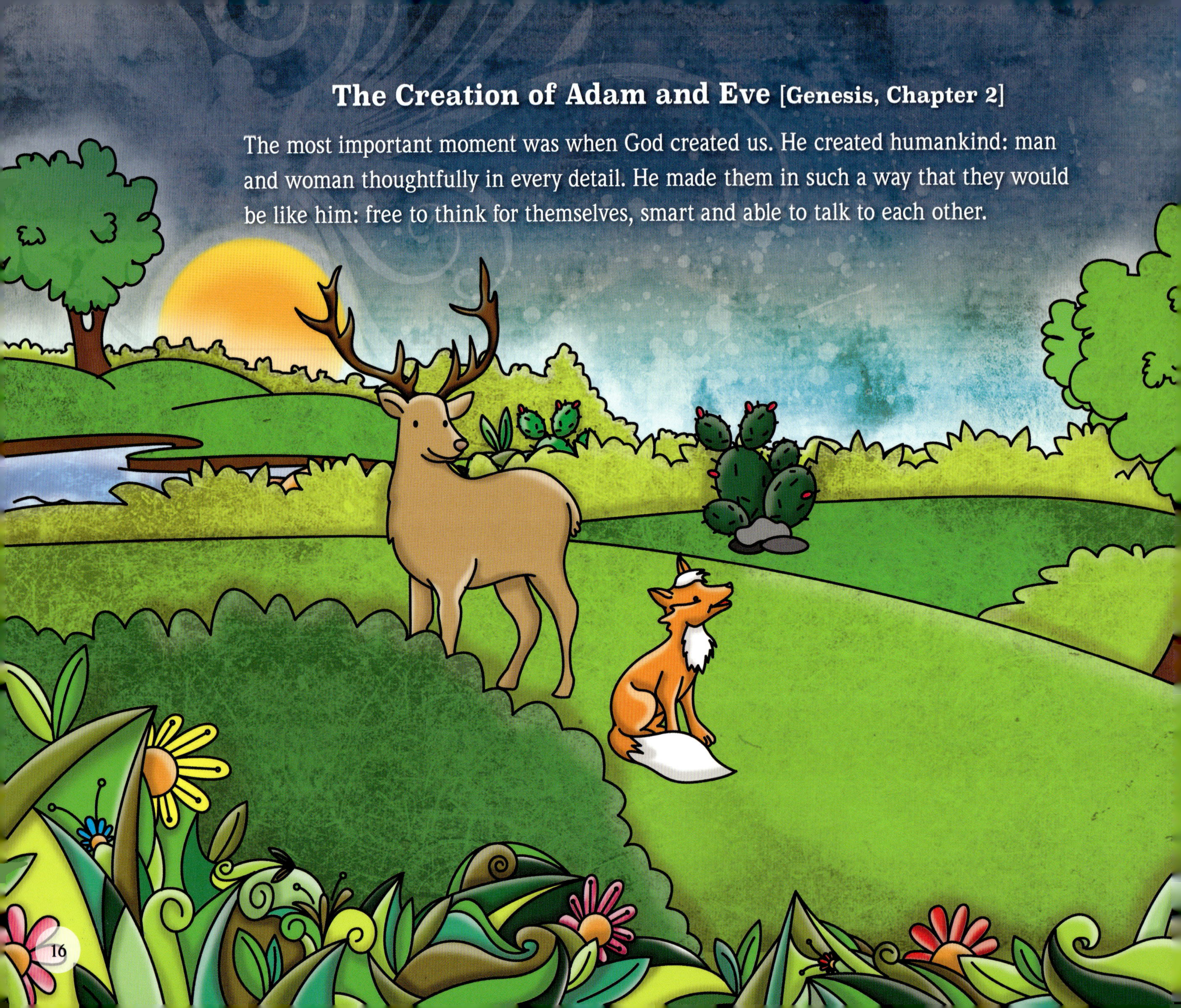

The Creation of Adam and Eve [Genesis, Chapter 2]

The most important moment was when God created us. He created humankind: man and woman thoughtfully in every detail. He made them in such a way that they would be like him: free to think for themselves, smart and able to talk to each other.

He gave them a beautiful place to live called Eden, which means "the garden of delights." Then he put them in charge of all that he had created. He told them to get married, to raise families, to love each other, and to be happy. God called the first man Adam, and Adam called the first woman Eve. Finally, after looking over all he had created, God saw that everything was good.

Original Sin [Genesis, Chapter 3]

Adam and Eve had everything they needed in the Garden of Eden. They had more than enough food, they were free from sickness or pain of any kind, and no evil was present in their hearts. They looked on each other with love and kindness. But there was a test that they had to pass: God asked them not to eat the fruit from just one tree, one that was in the middle of the garden. But Adam and Eve did not trust God, and as a result they were disobedient.

One day, when God came for his usual visit, he couldn't find Adam and Eve. They were hiding because they trusted a snake and were tricked into eating the fruit that God told them was forbidden....They were disobedient and felt ashamed, so they decided to hide. Their actions were selfish and brought sin into the world. This is known as "original sin." Adam and Eve passed this fault on to their children, and their children passed it on to their children. Now, because of this act of disobedience, we are born into sin.

Noah's Ark [Genesis, Chapter 7]

Adam and Eve did not trust God, and that made God sad. Because they didn't do what they were asked, Adam and Eve lost the beautiful place they had lived in. There were many who made bad choices and followed the dark path of sin, but some—like Noah's family—worked hard to help others and to please God. God asked Noah to build a large ship known as an "ark." He trusted and obeyed God even though some people made fun of him. There was a massive storm and big flood that covered the whole earth. All the good people who got on the ark were protected from the flood. Noah also saved lots of animals; he put a pair of every kind on the ark.

Abraham's Faith [Genesis, Chapter 22]

One person related to Noah was Abraham, whom we call our "father in the faith." One day God asked Abraham to leave his home so that God could show him a better place. Abraham didn't know where he was going, but he trusted God and traveled to what is known as the Promised Land. God gave Abraham many blessings. He gave him a son—even though Abraham and his wife, Sarah, were already very old and thought they couldn't have children. In this new land, they had everything they needed and were very happy. God promised that those who were descended—born from Abraham's family—would be as many as the stars in the sky and the grains of sand on the seashore!

The Sacrifice of Isaac [Genesis 22]

One day, though, the Lord called down from heaven: "Abraham, Abraham!" Abraham responded, "Here I am." God said to him, "Take your only son, Isaac, whom you love so much, and take him to the place that I will show to you. There, offer him to me as a sacrifice." In this way, Abraham was being tested to see if he would obey God's will. Abraham trusted and obeyed God again, even though what God asked would be very painful. But when he was at the point of sacrificing his son, which meant killing him, an angel of the Lord came down from heaven and stopped Abraham. Because he had obeyed God, God promised Abraham again that some day he would have many, many descendants.

Moses' Childhood [Exodus, Chapter 2]

Abraham's family grew a lot. After many years passed by, Abraham's grandson Jacob and his family had to leave the Promised Land. They all had to go to Egypt. Over time, Jacob's family grew so much that their numbers could not be counted. This is what God had promised Abraham. They were known as the People of Israel. Because there were so many Israelites, the pharaoh, or king of Egypt, was jealous and afraid of them.

He ordered his soldiers to kill every Israelite baby boy. Desperate to protect him, one Israelite woman put her baby in a little basket and left it floating in the river. The basket floated all the way to the palace of the pharaoh and was found by the princess who lived there when she went down to the river to take a bath. Even though the little baby was an Israelite, she decided to save him and bring him up in the court of her father, the pharaoh. She called him Moses, which means, "taken out of the water."

The Israelites Cross the Red Sea [Exodus, Chapter 14]

Time passed. When Moses was grown, God spoke to him—just like he had spoken to Abraham. The Lord asked Moses to free his people from the terrible slavery in which they lived in Egypt, and to take them back to the Promised Land. After celebrating their soon to be freedom, the Israelite families left, guided by Moses. The pharaoh, who was very angry, chased after them with his army.

They caught up with them and cornered them at the Red Sea. God opened a path through the middle of the water so the Israelites could pass through and escape. The pharaoh and his soldiers tried to follow them. But while they were still in the middle of the sea, God let the water close back up, and the Egyptians were drowned. The Israelites, however, were saved.

The Ten Commandments [Exodus, Chapter 20]

The Israelites continued to travel until they came to a very tall mountain that was called Mount Sinai. Moses went to the top of the mountain to meet with God and talk with him face to face, just like you talk to your friends. There, Moses received two stone tablets on which God himself had written the Ten Commandments. These were ten rules that helped the Israelites please God and be happy. Moses went down from Mount Sinai feeling good about God's support. He carried these stone tablets in his hands, and he went back to where the Israelites were camped.

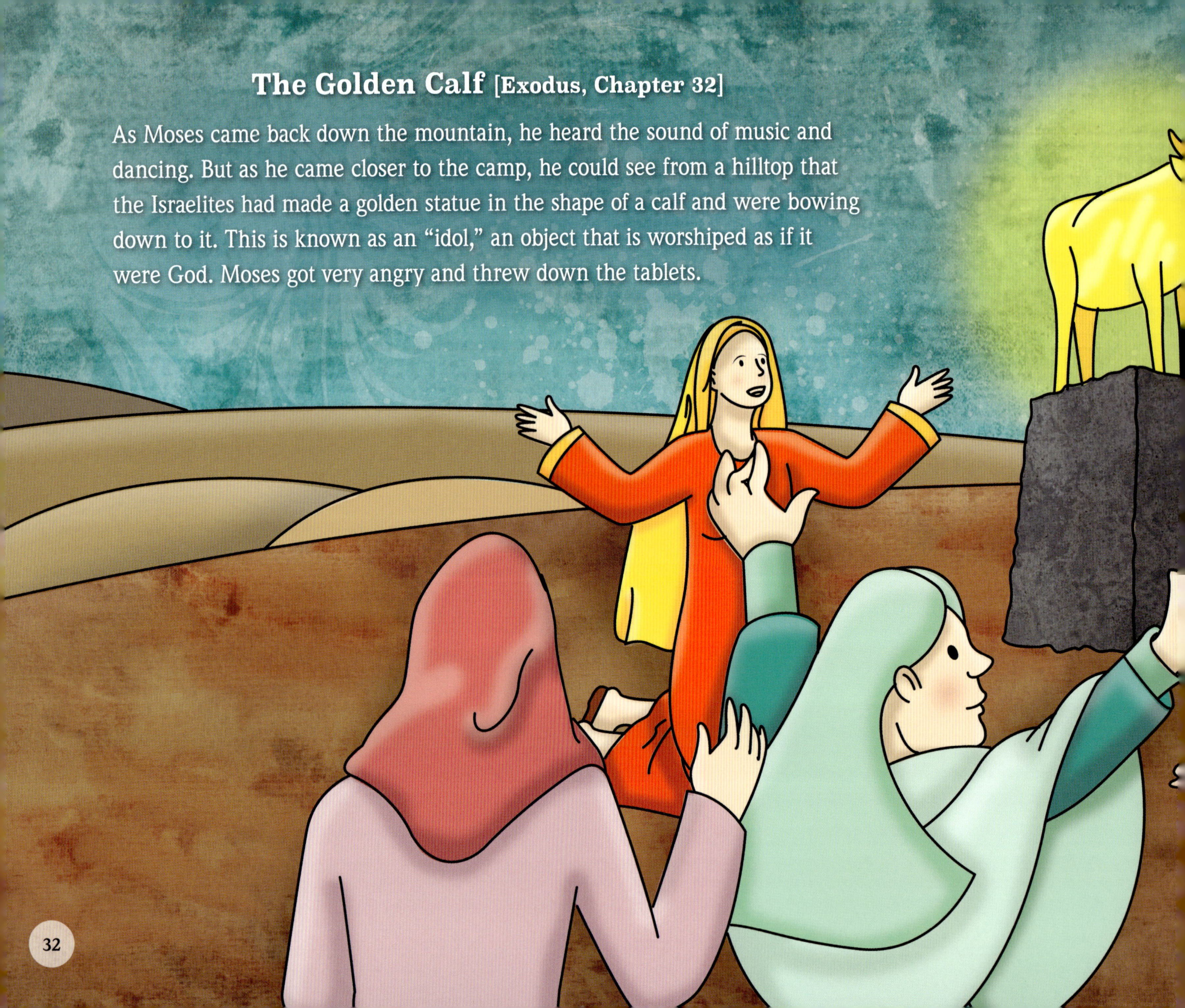

The Golden Calf [Exodus, Chapter 32]

As Moses came back down the mountain, he heard the sound of music and dancing. But as he came closer to the camp, he could see from a hilltop that the Israelites had made a golden statue in the shape of a calf and were bowing down to it. This is known as an "idol," an object that is worshiped as if it were God. Moses got very angry and threw down the tablets.

When they hit the ground, they broke into pieces in front of the Israelites. God became very unhappy because he had protected the Israelites for many years, and had just saved them from slavery in Egypt. In the end, the people were sorry for what they had done and God gave them new stone tablets on which the Ten Commandments were again written because he loved them very much.

David and Goliath [1 Samuel, Chapter 17]

The people of Israel spent a long time traveling in the desert before they finally got to the Promised Land, also called the Holy Land. They immediately settled in, excited and happy about their new home. After a little while the people began to pick the rich fruits of the land that God had given them. God chose a young shepherd named David to be the future king of his people. But long before the time came for him to become the king, he had to stand up for the whole nation of Israel and fight a terrible warrior named Goliath, who was much larger and stronger than David. The two fought, one against the other, each standing up for his own people: the Israelites against the Philistines. David beat Goliath by using his sling, a rock, and really good aim, but God's help was what made David able to win. With this victory God showed how much he loved his people and the Israelites knew that David was the chosen one of God.

The Wisdom of Solomon [1 Kings, Chapter 4]

King David wrote many hymns, or psalms, in honor of the Lord. David used those hymns to give thanks to God for his goodness, to ask his forgiveness, and also to ask for help. David chose the city of Jerusalem to be the capital of the Kingdom of Israel. He made it beautiful, and built his palace there. When David grew old and died, his son Solomon became the next king and built a wonderfully big

temple for God. He was a very wise man who knew how to solve many riddles and problems, but more than anything else, he was fair to others and defended the weak. He became so famous for his wisdom that kings and queens from far-off lands went to Jerusalem to meet him and to hear his wisdom.

The Prophets

Before Jesus became a man and came to the earth, God had spoken to us many times through the prophets. The prophets were ordinary persons whom God chose—as he had done before with Moses—to guide Israel with teachings that would keep them faithful to the Lord’s friendship.

When the people stopped keeping their promise to obey the Ten Commandments, God would send them a prophet. In God's name, the prophets told them that they were wrong and passed God's word on to them. Through those messages, God prepared his people, whom he loved so much, for the coming of his Son, Jesus.

The New Testament

Introduction to the New Testament

God was always faithful to the promise he made to Abraham and to all human beings. So, when he thought that everything was ready and that the right moment had come, he decided to send us Jesus. He sent him to us so we wouldn't have to listen to his messages only through religious leaders and prophets. Instead, his very own Son would share his messages with us! This is what the New Testament is about: Jesus and his message.

The Annunciation [Luke, Chapter 1]

There was a small city in the Holy Land called Nazareth. In it there lived a young woman named Mary who was married to a man named Joseph. He was a descendant from King David. One day, an angel of the Lord visited Mary; the angel's name was Gabriel. He told her, some very special news:

God had chosen her to become the mother of Jesus, our Savior. The Son of God wanted to become one of us so he could be with us on our way to God in heaven. Mary trusted God completely and agreed to become the mother of Jesus.

The Birth of Jesus [Luke, Chapter 2]

Several months later, the emperor Caesar Augustus ordered everyone in the land to go to the town from which their family came, where their names would be included in a census. Joseph traveled with Mary to Bethlehem, the home of his ancestor David. When they arrived in Bethlehem, the time came for Mary to give birth. Joseph couldn't find a room for them at the local inns, but he found a stable, where animals took shelter from the cold.

Mary gave birth there. There were a few shepherds nearby who were looking after their sheep that night. Some angels told them about the birth of Jesus, and as soon as they could, they went to meet the Baby Jesus. And so, together, both the angels and the shepherds proclaimed how happy they were on the day the Son of God was born.

The Magi

Some men called "Magi" who studied the stars also came from very far away to visit the Baby Jesus. They had seen a special star in the sky and, as soon as they learned that someone very important had been born, they rode their camels to Bethlehem and found the stable where Jesus was. Opening their gifts, they offered him gold, incense, and perfume. Mary and Joseph were very surprised by everything that was happening. And Mary kept all her feelings about these things in her heart.

The Killing of the Innocent Children [Matthew, Chapter 2]

When the Magi went back to their homes, they didn't go through Jerusalem, even though they had done so on the way to Bethlehem. King Herod asked them to stop by on their way back to tell him where to find the king of the Jews, as he called the Baby Jesus, so he could go to honor him, too, but what he really wanted to do was hurt Jesus. When Herod realized the Magi had returned to their countries without stopping to see him, Herod ordered his soldiers to kill all boys two years old or younger.

But Jesus wasn't in Bethlehem anymore. In fact, shortly before that happened, the angel of the Lord appeared in a dream to Joseph and told him to escape to Egypt with Mary and Jesus. They stayed there until King Herod died. When they finally returned to the Holy Land, they went to live in Nazareth.

Jesus Teaches in the Temple [Luke, Chapters 19, 21]

Jesus grew up and got stronger. The grace of God was in him. Every year, Jesus went up to Jerusalem with Mary and Joseph for the feast of Passover. When he was twelve years old, instead of going home to Nazareth with his parents, Jesus stayed in Jerusalem at the end of the celebrations. At first, Mary and Joseph didn't realize what Jesus had done. When they noticed he wasn't with them, they started to look for him. When they didn't find him, they returned to Jerusalem.

On the third day, they found him in the Temple, a very holy place, seated among its religious leaders. Jesus asked these leaders questions about the Bible and gave them the right answers to whatever they asked him. A little while later, the whole family went back to Nazareth. Jesus was a good son who respected and obeyed Mary and Joseph.

Jesus' Baptism [Matthew, Chapter 3]

Jesus, the Son of God, came to this world to tell us about the Kingdom of God and save us from our sins. When he was about thirty years old, he left his home and went to preach the Good News: God loved us so much that he sent his Son to visit us and teach us the way to heaven. When Jesus began to preach, he went to see John the Baptist to be baptized by him. While John was baptizing Jesus in the river Jordan, the heavens opened and the Holy Spirit appeared in the form of a dove. And the voice of God, the Father, was heard from heaven, saying, "This is my beloved Son, with whom I am well pleased."

The Wedding at Cana [John, Chapter 2]

One day there was a wedding being celebrated in a place called Cana, in Galilee, near the city where Jesus lived. Jesus and his disciples were there as guests, as was his mother, Mary. In the middle of the party, they ran out of wine. Mary noticed it and, very quietly, went to tell Jesus. Jesus asked the

servants to fill some stone jugs with water. Then an amazing thing happened. Jesus changed the water into wine. Thanks to this miracle, the wedding feast could go on. This was Jesus' first miracle. From that day on, his disciples believed in him much more.

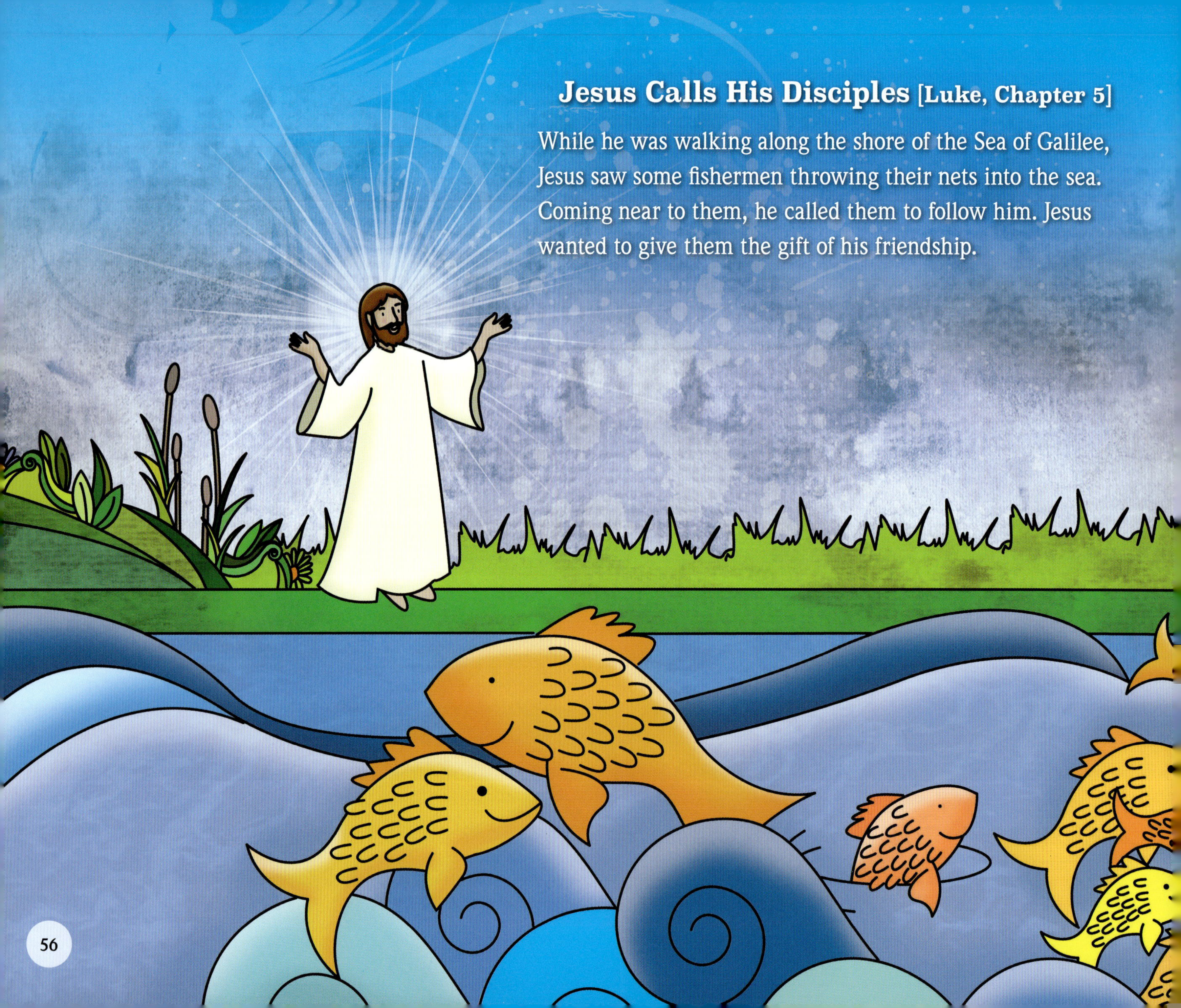

Jesus Calls His Disciples [Luke, Chapter 5]

While he was walking along the shore of the Sea of Galilee, Jesus saw some fishermen throwing their nets into the sea. Coming near to them, he called them to follow him. Jesus wanted to give them the gift of his friendship.

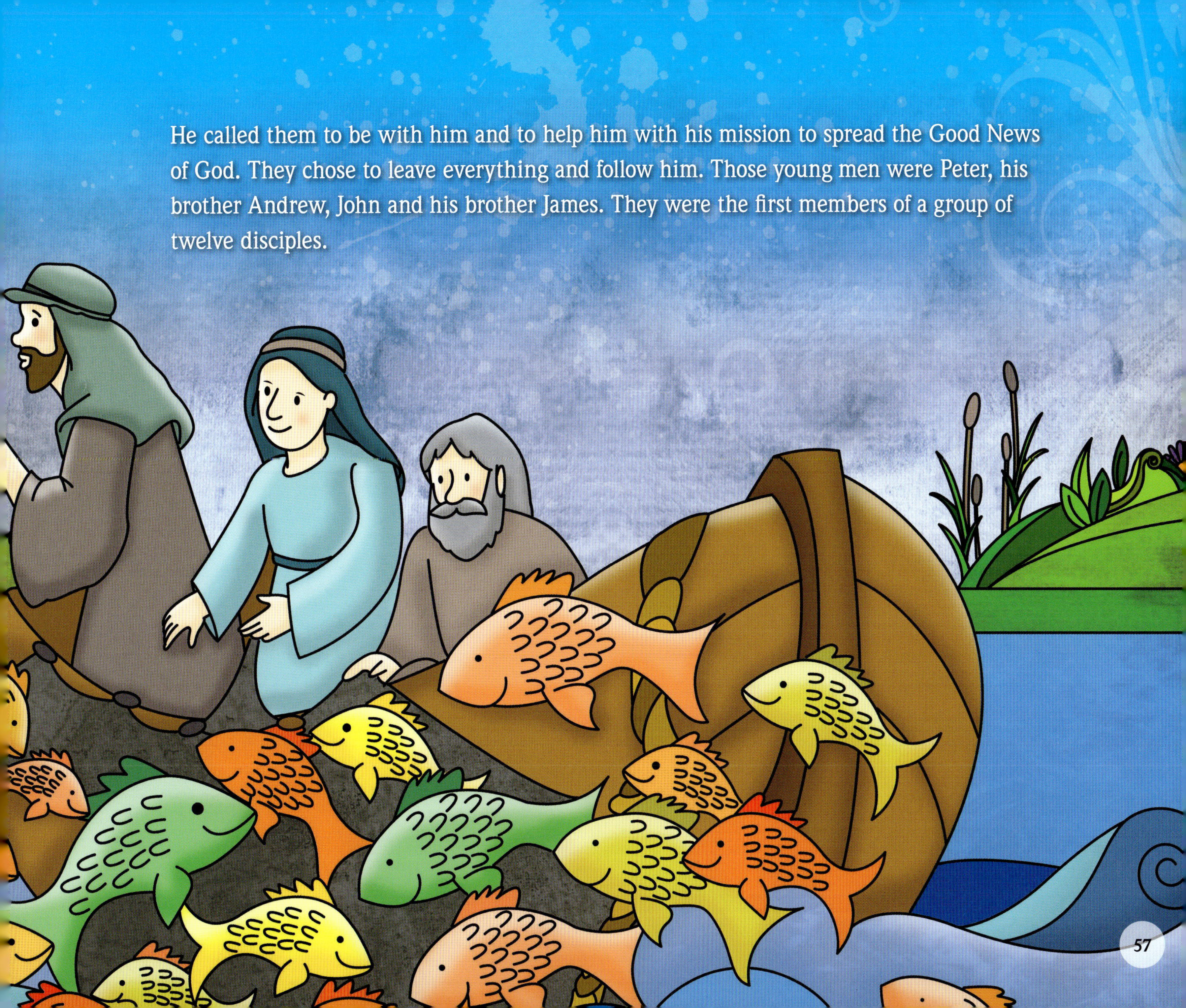

He called them to be with him and to help him with his mission to spread the Good News of God. They chose to leave everything and follow him. Those young men were Peter, his brother Andrew, John and his brother James. They were the first members of a group of twelve disciples.

The Resurrection of Lazarus [John, Chapter 11]

Among the friends that Jesus made while he was living in Israel telling all about the Good News was a young man named Lazarus. His two sisters were Martha and Mary. When Lazarus got very sick they sent for Jesus, but he died before Jesus arrived. His sisters felt very sad and went looking for Jesus. When he heard of his friend's death, Jesus began to cry.

When he arrived at the tomb where the body of Lazarus had been laid, Jesus cried out in a loud voice, "Lazarus, come out!" To the surprise of everyone, Lazarus did. He came back to life! In fact, Jesus had said that he was the resurrection and the life. That's why whoever believes in Jesus, even though we die, will live.

Jesus Calms a Storm [Mark, Chapter 4]

One time Jesus was crossing the Sea of Galilee in a boat with his disciples. Jesus was lying down, resting from a hard day. Soon, he drifted off to sleep. Suddenly, a dreadful storm began. The disciples, who were very scared, went to Jesus and said to him, "Master, wake up! We are going to sink!" Jesus got up and scolded the storm, saying, "Be quiet; calm down!" Right away the wind and the sea got quiet. Everybody was amazed, and said, "Who is this, that even the wind and the sea obey him?"

The Multiplication of the Bread and Fish [Matthew, Chapter 14]

One day, Jesus was talking to a large crowd of people. Time went by quickly, and before they knew it, it was late afternoon. Most of the people hadn't had anything to eat. Jesus' disciples went up to him and asked him to send the people away. But Jesus felt sorry for them because these people had been with him for a long time, and most would have to walk a long way back on an empty stomach.

So Jesus asked everyone to sit down. In the meantime, a young boy brought him five loaves of bread and two fish. Jesus took them and raising his eyes up to God, his Father, blessed the food, broke it up, and gave it to his disciples. They, in turn, handed the pieces out to everybody else. All ate until they were full, and they even filled some baskets with leftovers.

The Lords' Prayer [Matthew, Chapter 6]

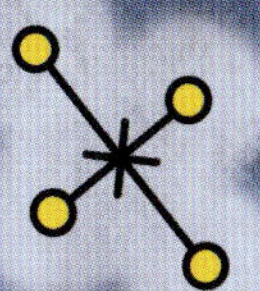

One of the people who were following Jesus saw him one day while he was praying and was very impressed. So he asked Jesus to teach them to pray. Jesus taught him that God is our Father, and that we should trust in him and say, "Our Father who art in heaven, hallowed be thy name. Thy kingdom come. Thy will be done on earth, as it is in heaven. Give us this day our daily bread, and forgive us our trespasses, as we forgive those who trespass against us, and lead us not into temptation, but deliver us from evil."

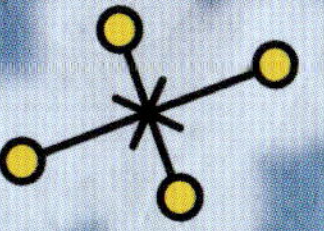

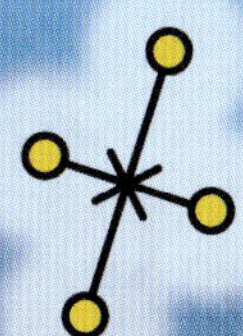

Jesus Throws the Merchants Out of the Temple [Matthew, Chapter 21]

One day when Jesus went to the Temple to pray he saw a lot of merchants at the Temple entrance selling things. He saw them being greedy and unfair to the poor, so he threw them out.

He told them not to do that in the Temple because it was a holy place, “a place of prayer.” Many people didn’t understand what Jesus did, and many were angry with him.

The Parable of the Prodigal Son [Luke, Chapter 15]

Everyone drew close to Jesus, especially the people who knew the bad things they had done and who wanted to be better. One time he told them this story: A young man asked his father for his part of the property he was to inherit from him. Then he took off to a place far away where he wasted all he had been given until he ended up with nothing, not even food to eat. Looking for a way to earn money, the only work he found was taking care of pigs.

After some time, he felt ashamed by how he had treated his family. Feeling sorry in his heart, he started the journey home. Instead of scolding him about his bad choices, his father hugged and kissed him, and threw a party to celebrate his return. God is like this; he waits for us to return to his loving embrace.

Jesus Is the Good Shepherd [John, Chapter 10]

Jesus called himself the "good shepherd." A good shepherd cares for his sheep, treating them with tender care and protecting them from harm. He is even willing to give his life for them.

We are Jesus' "sheep." And so it is that Jesus said if one of us gets lost he will always go looking for us, no matter if it puts him in danger. When he finds us he will heal our wounds and bring us back to the rest of the flock. Everyone in heaven is happy each time Jesus finds a lost person.

Jesus Enters Jerusalem

Once, Jesus went to Jerusalem, the holy city, to celebrate the feast of Passover with his friends. When the people heard he was there, they wanted to welcome him.

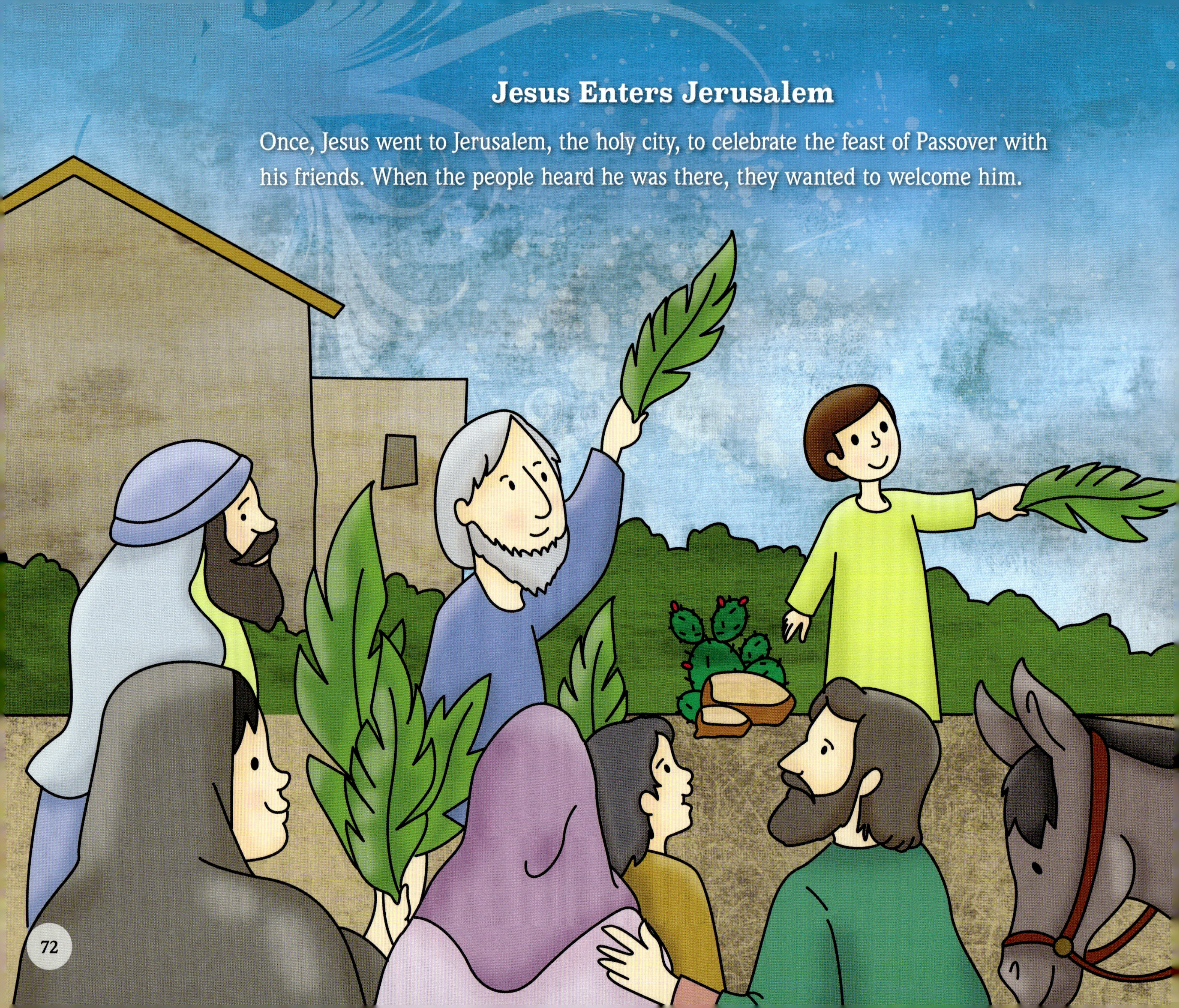

A very large crowd came to see him, waving olive branches and spreading their cloaks out on the street. He entered Jerusalem riding on a donkey. And everyone who was there shouted, "Blessed is he who comes in the name of the Lord!"

The Last Supper [Luke, Chapter 22]

Jesus loved us so much that he even wanted to give his life for us. When the time came for him to go back to God, his Father in heaven, he left a sign of his love for us. At the Passover dinner, Jesus took bread in his hands, broke it, and gave it to his disciples, saying, "Take and eat;

this is my body." And he did the same with the cup of wine, saying, "This is my blood." Then, he said, "Do this in memory of me." This was the first Mass, when he gave us the gift of the Eucharist.

The Prayer in the Garden [Matthew, Chapter 26]

After the Last Supper, Jesus went to a garden with his disciples to pray. While he prayed, Jesus felt very afraid of the pain and death that were waiting for him. In the middle of that great fear he spoke

these words to God, his Father: "Father, if it is possible, take these sufferings away from me. But not my will, but yours be done." It was already getting late and the disciples were so tired that they fell asleep. Jesus became even sadder because he began to feel very lonely.

Judas' Betrayal [Matthew, Chapter 26]

Jesus had just finished praying when some guards showed up and arrested him. Judas, one of Jesus' friends, told them where to find Jesus. He received thirty silver coins for the information. Judas said to the guards, "Come. I will show you where Jesus is. I will kiss him so you will know him." And when they arrived at the garden, Judas did just that. The guards arrested Jesus by force and took him to prison. There, the governor, Pontius Pilate, ordered him to be beaten with a whip until his whole body was covered with cuts.

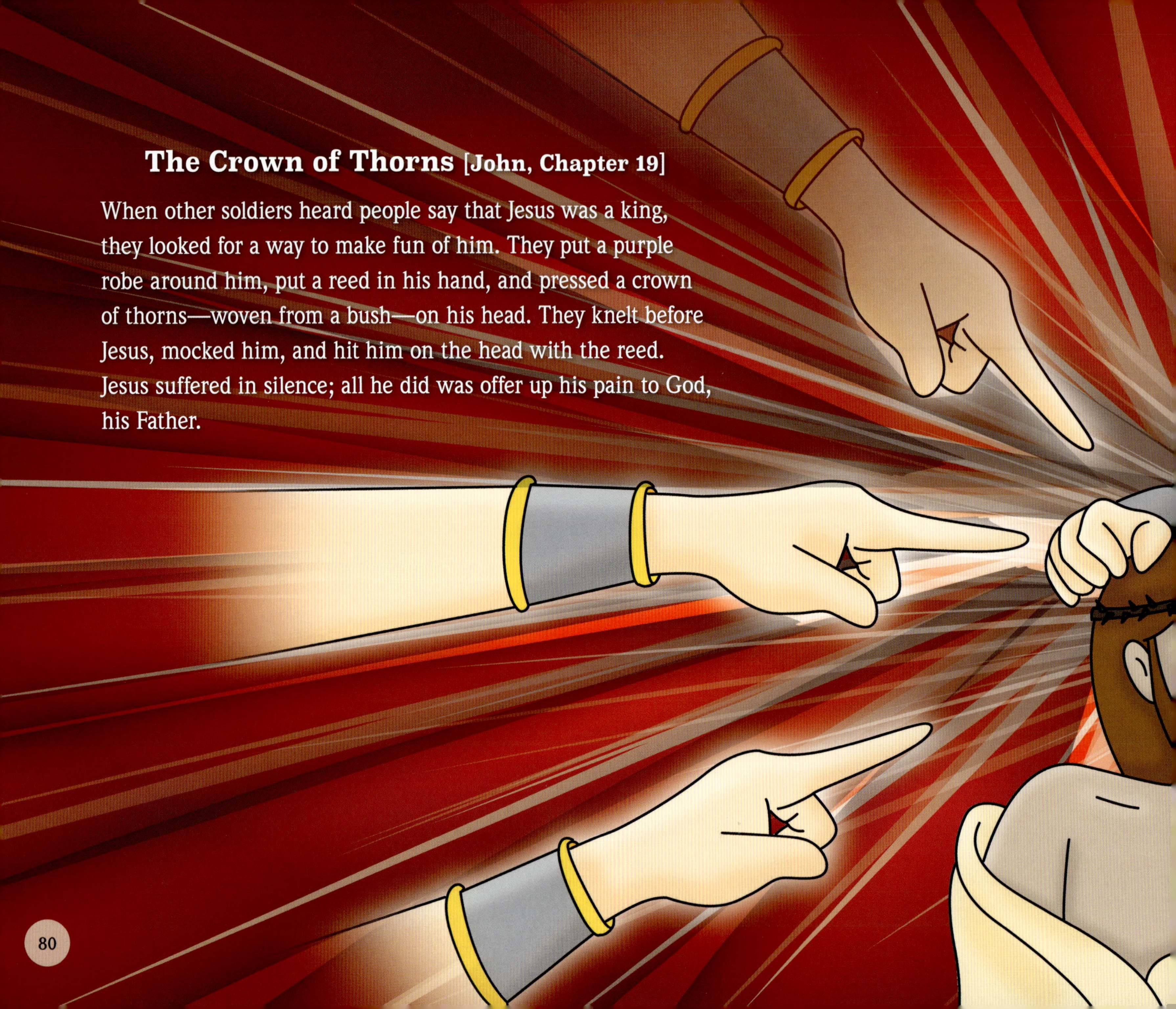

The Crown of Thorns [John, Chapter 19]

When other soldiers heard people say that Jesus was a king, they looked for a way to make fun of him. They put a purple robe around him, put a reed in his hand, and pressed a crown of thorns—woven from a bush—on his head. They knelt before Jesus, mocked him, and hit him on the head with the reed. Jesus suffered in silence; all he did was offer up his pain to God, his Father.

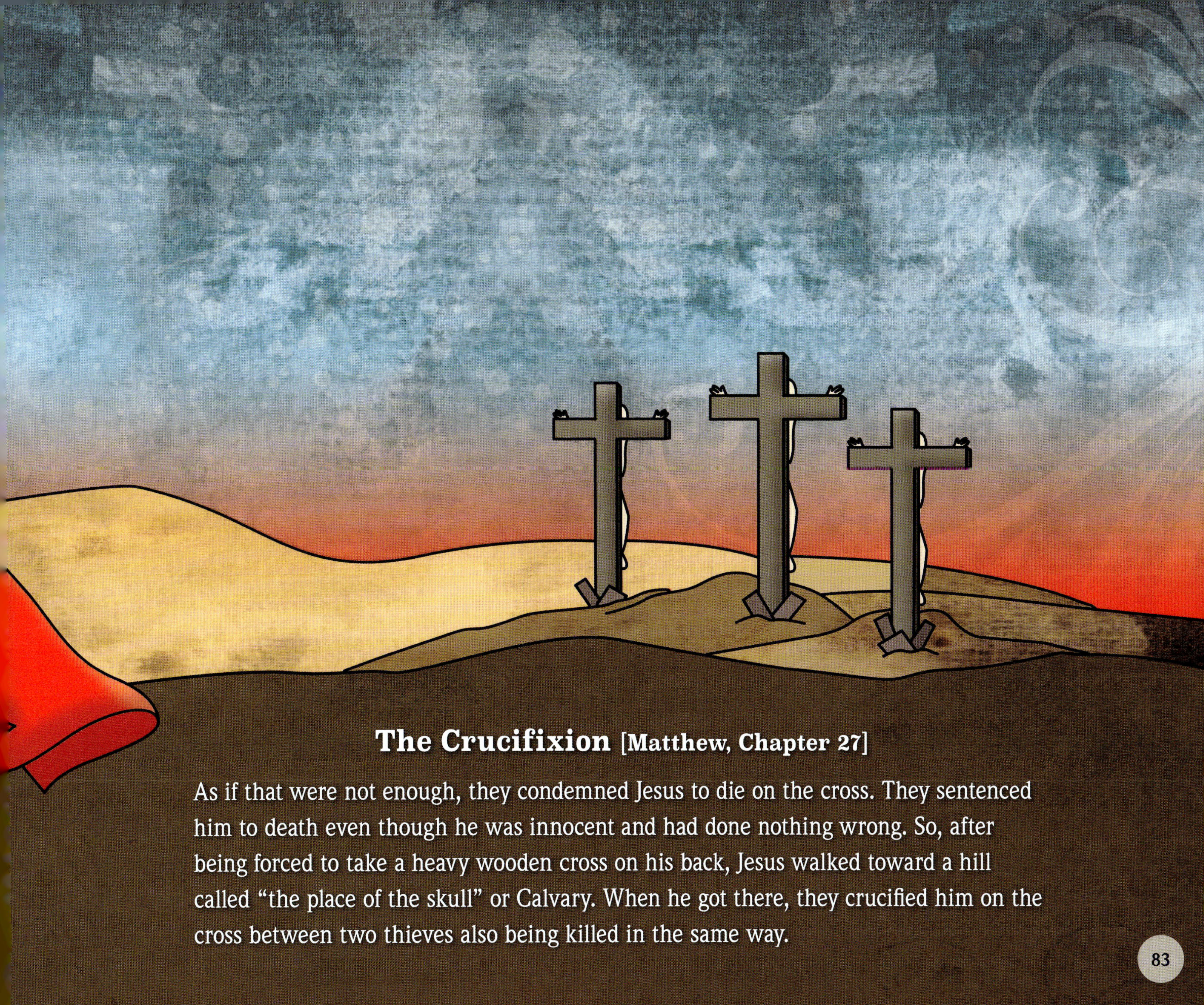

The Crucifixion [Matthew, Chapter 27]

As if that were not enough, they condemned Jesus to die on the cross. They sentenced him to death even though he was innocent and had done nothing wrong. So, after being forced to take a heavy wooden cross on his back, Jesus walked toward a hill called "the place of the skull" or Calvary. When he got there, they crucified him on the cross between two thieves also being killed in the same way.

Jesus' Body Is Taken Down from the Cross

After suffering on the cross for hours, Jesus handed his life over to God, his Father, and died. Then one of the soldiers there came and thrust a sharp weapon called a lance into the side of Jesus' body. From his side flowed blood and water. When he saw this, the soldier said, "This man was truly the Son of God."

Nearby were Jesus' Mother, Mary; John, the disciple; Mary Magdalene, and other women. They took his body down from the cross and put it in a tomb that had been carved out of rock. They covered the door with a very big round stone and left.

The Resurrection [Luke, Chapter 24]

But death was not the end for Jesus. On Sunday, Mary Magdalene, who loved Jesus very much, got up early in the morning and went to the tomb. She wanted to anoint the body of Jesus. When she arrived at the place where they had buried him, she saw that the stone over the tomb's door was no longer in its place. Angels dressed in white said to her, "Why are you looking among the dead for someone who is alive? He is not here. He is risen!"

Jesus Appears to the Disciples [Luke, Chapter 24]

Meanwhile, the apostles of Jesus had been staying locked in the same room where they had held the Last Supper with him. They were afraid that people might hurt them too because they were followers of Jesus. Even though the doors were locked, Jesus appeared in the middle of the group and said, "Peace be with you!"

They were scared and thought that he was a ghost. But he showed them his pierced hands and side and invited them to touch him. It was really Jesus! He was alive again! This made them very happy.

The Disciples of Emmaus [Luke, Chapter 24]

After Jesus had risen from the dead, he was alive in a new way. After Jesus died, two disciples, who lived in a little town not far from Jerusalem, were returning home. A stranger greeted them. It was Jesus, but they didn't know that. They told him they were sad. Jesus listened to them. When they arrived at their town, the disciples invited Jesus to stay with them because it was getting late in the day. Jesus accepted, and entered their house. He sat down at the table with them, took some bread, broke it and gave it to them. Suddenly, they knew who he was. They realized he had been with them from the moment they met him on the road. They felt their hearts fill with joy.

The Ascension into Heaven [Acts, Chapter 1]

For forty days, Jesus kept appearing to his friends, here and there. Finally, he called them together on a mountain near Jerusalem. As he blessed them, Jesus went up to heaven. At last, he went home to God, his Father! Even so, Jesus Christ is always with us—through his word, and especially through his Real Presence in the Eucharist.

The Coming of the Holy Spirit [Acts, Chapter 2]

After Jesus went back to his Father in heaven, the disciples returned to Jerusalem. Jesus had told them to wait for strength from above through the Holy Spirit. They waited in prayer together with Mary, the Mother of Jesus. When the feast of Pentecost came, there was a loud noise like that of a strong wind, and something like "tongues of fire" appeared.

A flame came to rest on each one of the people who had gathered, and they were all filled with the Holy Spirit. It was the love of God that was poured into their hearts. Made strong by that love, they went out to the entire world to tell everyone that Jesus was alive!